Roxanne the Green Nose Reindeer

Jason R. Van Pelt

Copyright © 2021 Jason R. Van Pelt

All rights reserved. No part of this book may be reproduced or transmitted in any form or by any means, electronic or mechanical, including photocopying, recording or by any information storage and retrieval system without permission in writing from the publisher.

J.R.V.P—Madison, WI
ISBN: 978-1-7371572-9-8
Library of Congress Control Number: 2021919576
Title: *Roxanne the Green Nose Reindeer*
Author: Jason R. Van Pelt
Digital distribution | 2021
Paperback | 2021

This is a work of fiction. The characters, names, incidents, places, and dialogue are products of the author's imagination, and are not to be construed as real.

Dedication

To the harmony of the American community for all.

Before joining Santa Jay Claus, Sandy May Claus, and all the reindeer of our Happy Holiday Legion.
Roxanne The Green Nose Reindeer had wintry adventures of her own in the Antarctica region.

A favoring for a workaday worldling would be a savoring of polar magnetosphere illuminescence.
Lo! A wonderful visually exciting aurora lighting of northern, southern, and earthern quintessence...

The North Pole has various divisions of elves working around the clock yearlong entirely in preparation.
They're inventing, tinkering, painting, sculpting, molding, and welding folks a Christmas reparation.

'Tis a moment to be decent among society moreover than the rest of the earlier months memorably recent.
This polarized precedent of a wintertime fait accompli is very relevant, evident, and yes heaven-sent.

Fellow equal people celebrate our holiday by treating one another withal kindness, grace, & giving.
Few of the elves were experimenting then made a toy called, "*The Alienator*" which alienates everything.

It is a handheld device transmitting a green ray outward forward toward any aimed within range target.
Testing this prototype on each other hence becoming aliens suddenly taking the toy gun off the market.

Knowing what Santa Jay Claus would say, "*Guns are not toys*", they get ready to flee southward.
Shooting n' transforming an extra sleigh into an UFO faster than reindeer as well as an ostrich bird.

Early evening on Christmas Eve many wide eyed Antarcticans saw a strange flying saucer hard to believe.
Scientists stationed at the research outpost of Antarctica dispatch to investigate whence they conceive.

Their technological devices are malfunctioning alike the Bermuda Triangle as the space between lessens.
Haywire now an only thing left working is the green aura spreading some alienating transgressions.

The humans are abducted and transmogrified ergo walking talking aliens in cahoots with alien elves.
All this ruckus got the undivided attention of The Green Nose Reindeer Roxanne thus she delves.

Reaching the alienated site Roxanne finds cover beneath a snowbank preserving hearing distance.
Screeching sounds are their alien language and they're formulating world domination unless resistance.

An alien elf notices a green glow outshining thereon the environs whilst piloting a mini UFO saucer.
Roxanne flexes her hooves soaring upward following her nose away from this alienated elf double crosser.

A chase soon ensues neither of whom wants to lose as the ruse of a race pursues across the South Pole.
They cruise through midair doing flips and nosedive dips yet such a dare to choose to use a barrel roll.

Ahoy! She speeds up full of Christmas magic then zigzags never getting jet lags she brags and tail wags.
Zipping by frozen crags her fur coat is fluffing akin to soft clean rags of brand new tags safely as air bags.

Outflanked as well as out of fuel the spacecraft comes to a sudden stop picking a spot it emergency lands.
There Roxanne stands at the door of the small UFO shining her wintergreen nose upon those alien glands.

After a grueling grizzly grabble of a grumble that pilot starts to stumble dizzily then takes a tumble.
Her green nosy bright light is purifying so the alienation of this elf fades off and begins a crumble.

An interrogation is called for in order to discover truths about what's going on here to finally settle.
Antarctican penguins alongside Roxanne get an explanation thereby their normalized elf of mettle.

The situation is urgent and as dangerous as a shark tank, a pirate plank, or an icicle clank melting.
Not much time until nightfall approaches therefore these aliens have to be thwarted from pelting.
Flocks of penguins swim intending to help Roxanne ambush the alien threat thereafter stabilize.

Two large alien scientists are guarding outside of the main UFO at this point it does sensationalize.
They've been busy constructing a mothership designed for destructing all of the Christmas tradition.
Obstructing an original tiding by gently abducting gifts of close families confiding an enriching addition.

Green nose Roxanne blends in amongst the flashing lights and nuzzles her nose to save those humans.
Rays of alienating greenness pummel her fur howbeit she's immune to the way the Alienator illumines.

Hundreds of penguins burst up belly first surrounding the couple of remaining aliens whom eschew.
Wafting north athwart the equator speeding erewhile Roxanne rockets right there behind them ado!

Nearer her green nose reverts most of what the Alienator did and the UFO crashes in New Mexico.
Joy! The unapproved toy instantly destroyed and arctic elves back to themselves like how we know.

Hark! She's indisputably altogether the doughty leader of the South Pole enacting a masterful plan.
Christmas holiday is forever a go-go receiving the green light thanks to the manifesto of Roxanne.

Her heroic heart, Christmas spirit, magnificent mind, and soul lays in bed sipping a warm soup bowl.
For many moons Roxanne the Green Nose Reindeer has dreamt about the good ole North Pole!

Other books by Jason R. Van Pelt

www.ingramcontent.com/pod-product-compliance
Lightning Source LLC
Chambersburg PA
CBHW051259110526

44589CB00025B/2879